A baked jacket potato will keep hot for up to three hours in one of the wide necked food flasks. Remember to pack butter, cheese, salt and a fork.

D1515881

Since vacuum flasks are designed to keep food almost at its original temperature, they can be used for carrying cold things in hot weather – icecream, salads and cold drinks are all good ideas.

Contents

Note:

For the purposes of this book, 25 g = 1 oz and 500 ml = 1 pint.
A teaspoon = 5 ml and a tablespoon = 15 ml.

First edition

© LADYBIRD BOOKS LTD MCMLXXXIII

Packed
Lunches

by KATE HUTCHINSON
photographs by TIM CLARK

Ladybird Books Loughborough

Sandwiches

Sandwiches were named after the Earl of Sandwich who was a keen card player. He became so absorbed in the game that he asked for slices of meat to be placed between bread so that he could eat and play cards at the same time.

Sandwiches are convenient to eat and easy to make, so they are ideal for packed lunches. They can however be both dry and uninteresting, so to start with, remember to –

Use really *fresh* bread

Use *different* kinds of bread to introduce variety –
   white, brown, granary and best of all wholewheat

Use *softened* butter or margarine

Cover bread *right up to the edge* with the chosen
   filling

Earl's Sandwich

1 Cut some bread thinly or take 2-4 slices from a cut loaf and spread sparingly with softened butter or margarine.

2 Place slices of cold meat (ham, beef, chicken, pork) on one piece of bread and sprinkle with a little salt. Spread with mustard if liked.

3 Cover with another piece of bread and cut into quarters.

4 Don't cut off the crusts (except for very special parties) because it is a waste.

5 Wrap immediately in cling film or aluminium foil
to keep the sandwiches fresh.

Include a stick of celery or firm tomato to eat with
the sandwiches. They will provide a different
texture, and help to make sure that the meal is
nutritionally balanced.

Sandwiches printed in pink (opposite) will freeze and store for up to four weeks when carefully wrapped.

Smørrebrød

Children in Denmark take traditional open sandwiches *(smørrebrød)* to school wrapped in foil in their lunch boxes. Why don't you try some for a change?

Slices of rye bread or granary are best to use, but for a change use a bap or thick white bread buttered.

The fillings should be very mixed and very decorative with garnishes on top to suit your own personal tastes.

Here are some ideas to start you off, but you can probably think of many more.

Slice of corned beef with potato salad and watercress

Slice of processed cheese with a round of tinned pineapple and a radish flower in the middle

Roll a slice of ham around some grated carrot and coconut and garnish with cress

Cottage or cream cheese with orange segments and halved grapes

Whole sardine on a lettuce leaf garnished with sliced hard-boiled egg

Slices of salami, overlapped alternately with slices of cucumber on top of a slice of cheese

Garnishes

Cucumber slices

Cucumber cornets

Beetroot dice

Orange half curls

Radish flowers

Spring onion tassels

Lemon butterflies

French Flute

1 Split a fresh French stick lengthways, leaving a hinge along one side.

2 Spread with herb butter (opposite).

3 Fill along the whole length of the stick with various sorts of salami.

4 Add crisp lettuce hearts.

5 Slice into diagonal slices.

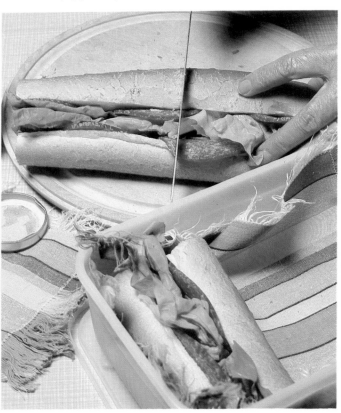

Herb Butter

*75 g (3 oz) softened
  butter*

*5 ml (teaspoonful)
  chopped fresh herbs*

*5 ml (teaspoonful) lemon
  juice*

Paprika pepper

Put all the ingredients into a basin and beat
thoroughly with a wooden spoon until light and fluffy.

Stuffed French Loaf

1 thickish French loaf (sometimes called a baton)

3 chopped hard-
boiled eggs
2 cups chopped
cooked ham or
chicken
1 cup diced cheese
Some chopped
chives or parsley
1 cup salad cream
½ pkt powdered
gelatine
Salt and pepper

1 Cut the loaf into two long pieces.
2 Scoop out the soft centres of each half without breaking through the crust to make 2 hollow tubes. (Brown the crumbs in the oven and use for Scotch eggs.)
3 Mix together the ham, eggs, cheese and chives in one basin.
4 Dissolve the gelatine in a little water according to the instructions on the packet, and stir into the salad cream.
5 Stir the two mixtures together, and add salt and black pepper if needed.
6 Spoon into the hollow half loaves and join together to make one long loaf.
7 Wrap tightly in plastic film or foil and refrigerate for 2-3 hours until set.
8 Serve, cut into slices.

Batch Sandwiches

If you have a deep freeze, try making a whole lot of sandwiches at a time – enough for two weeks perhaps. It saves time in the morning, it ensures really fresh bread, and it avoids waste by using up a whole tin or packet of filling whilst it is fresh.

Sandwiches taken out of the deep freeze at breakfast time will be thawed and ready to eat in time for lunch.

*1 wholemeal loaf
(thinly sliced)
1 large white sliced loaf
200g (8oz) butter or margarine*

*4 different fillings
that will freeze
(see the ones in
pink on page 6)*

1 Prepare the fillings in four separate basins.
2 Spread all the slices of bread with butter.
3 Put all white bread slices on the table top and use the fillings to make four kinds of sandwiches.
4 Place brown slices of bread on top.
5 Press gently but firmly. Cut into quarters.
6 Wrap up into individual packets with cling film or foil or freezer bags.
7 Label, date and freeze.

Triple Decker Sandwiches

1 Layer different sorts, but same sized, slices of buttered bread with three different fillings.

e.g. crunchy peanut butter and orange slices
watercress and cream cheese
liver pâté

2 Press gently together.
3 Cut down in 1¼ cm (½ inch) slices through all the layers.

For a party

Use an unsliced loaf.

Cut off all the crusts and cut into slices lengthways.

Spread with butter and chosen fillings.

Reassemble into loaf shape.

Wrap tightly and chill for 2-6 hours.

Slice when needed, and serve flat on a plate to show the different layers and colours.

Sandwiches don't have to be square, try these!

Pinwheels

1 Cut all the crusts off a large unsliced sandwich loaf and cut thin slices from the side, making long slices of bread.

2 Spread with margarine or softened butter and then with any creamed or mashed filling.

3 Starting at the narrow end, roll up the slice. Repeat with all the slices and then wrap up in foil or cling film and chill.

4 When ready to serve, unwrap and cut into 1¼ cm (½ inch) slices, making pinwheels.

Two suggested fillings
Sardine and Parsley

1 tin sardines mashed and mixed with 10 ml (2 teaspoonfuls) lemon juice

Some chopped parsley
Salt and pepper

Cheese and Chives

1 pkt cream cheese
1 small clove garlic crushed (optional)
15 ml (1 tablespoonful) chopped chives or spring onion tops
Pinch each of thyme and salt and pepper

Sandwich Toasties

Most sandwiches, except those with green salad
inside them, toast well. Toasted sandwiches can be
toasted in three ways.

1 You can toast sandwiches under an ordinary grill.
Make the sandwiches with plenty of filling and
press together lightly.

Set the grill on the highest setting and allow to
get hot for 2-3 minutes.

Place the sandwiches to be toasted on the rack
and grill until browned, turn over and grill the
other side.

Cut into triangles and serve with wedges of
tomato and salad.

2 If you have an infra-red contact grill, make the
   sandwiches as before, then set the cooker at the
   highest setting.

   Place the sandwiches on the bottom plate and
   close the grill.

   Cook until nicely browned, 2-3 minutes, turning
   the sandwich 90° to make an interesting criss-
   cross pattern.

3 If you have a sandwich toaster, just follow the
   instructions in the booklet that comes with it.
   BUT –

Remember that because the sandwiches are sealed at
the edges, steam from the filling is trapped, so
don't burn your mouth!

Pasties

The tin miners of Cornwall had very dirty jobs and so their wives made pasties that they could hold in one hand wrapped in a cloth. The traditional shape of a Cornish pasty is ideal to fit into a man's hand. As he ate the pasty the cloth was pulled down, rather as we unskin a banana when we eat it. The ingredients are a mixture of meat and vegetables in a pastry case, making a balanced meal all in one.

If you are fed up with sandwiches, why not try pasties instead? The pastry recipe is given first.

Shortcrust Pastry

200g (8oz) plain flour
Pinch of salt
50g (2oz) lard

50g (2oz) block margarine
50ml (3½ tablespoonfuls)
iced water

All spoon measurements should be levelled carefully with a knife.

Remember – to make successful pastry, measurements *must* be accurate and hands, equipment and ingredients *must* be as cool as possible. Start by washing your hands in cold water.

1 Sieve flour and salt into mixing bowl and add lard and margarine cut up into little pieces.

2 Rub lard and margarine into flour, using fingertips, until mixture looks like breadcrumbs.

3 Add all the water at once and mix with a knife.

4 Gather mixture together, with hand, into a firm piece of dough.

5 Use at once or put into polythene bag in a cool place until needed (it will keep 3-4 days in fridge).

This basic shortcrust pastry can be used to make all the dishes on pages 20-27, any of which may be eaten either hot *or* cold.

Cornish Pasties

Basic quantity of
   shortcrust pastry
150g (6oz) corned beef
   cut in one thick slice
   and cubed
1 medium potato

1 medium carrot
1 small onion
1 stick celery (optional)
5 ml (teaspoonful) salt
   and few shakes pepper
A little milk for glazing

1 Light oven on Gas Mark 6 (Electricity
   400°F/200°C).

2 Peel vegetables and cut into dice.

3 Put into boiling salted water (5 ml salt) and cook
   for just 8 minutes.

4 Make shortcrust pastry whilst vegetables are
   cooking unless you prepared this before.

5 Strain vegetables and allow to cool, then add
   cubed beef and a few shakes of pepper.

6 Divide pastry into four equal pieces.

7 Roll each piece thinly on a floured table.

8 Using a saucer as a guide, cut one circle from each piece of pastry.

9 Gather trimmings together, re-roll and cut one more circle.

10 Divide filling into five, and pile one portion in centre of each circle of pastry.

11 Brush edge of half of each pastry circle with water.

12 Fold in half with edges together, and pinch to seal.

13 Flute edge to decorate.

14 Brush with milk to glaze.

15 Bake 20-25 minutes until golden brown.

Other pasty fillings
Cheese and Onion

100g (4oz) Cheddar cheese
1 small onion
A little cold mashed potato (optional)

Pinch of herbs
15ml (1 tablespoonful) milk

Grate cheese and onion and add other ingredients.

Kipper and Egg

1 pkt boil-in-the-bag kippers

2 hard-boiled eggs

Cook kippers as directed.

Snip open bag, skin and bone fish (but use the juices)

Add to chopped hard-boiled eggs.

Sausage Rolls

Basic quantity of
   shortcrust pastry (or
   frozen puff pastry –
   thawed)

200g (8oz) sausage
   meat or skinned
   sausages
A little milk for glazing

1 Light oven on Gas Mark 6 (Electricity
   400°F/200°C).

2 Make pastry.

3 Shape into an oblong and then roll carefully, keeping it a good oblong shape until it measures approximately 35 cm × 25 cm (14 in × 10 in).

4 Using the rolling pin as a ruler, cut the pastry in half lengthwise.

5 Divide sausage meat in half and shape into two long sausages the same length as the pastry (use a little flour if sticky).

6 Place one long sausage down outside edge of each piece of pastry.

7 Brush along cut edge of pastry with water.

8 Roll the pastry over the sausage, starting from the outside edge and making sure the join is underneath.

9 Brush with milk to glaze.

10 Cut each long roll into six or eight sausage rolls.

11 Snip top of each to allow heat to penetrate.

12 Place on baking sheet.

13 Bake for 20 minutes until golden brown.

Savoury Tartlets (makes 12)

Basic quantity of
  shortcrust pastry
125 ml (¼ pt) milk
1 egg (size 3 or 4)
1 rasher bacon
1 small onion

1 mushroom (optional)
75 g (3 oz) grated cheese
2.5 ml (½ level
  teaspoonful) salt
Few shakes of pepper
A little oil or lard

1 Light oven on Gas Mark 5 (Electricity
  375°F/190°C).

2 Peel onion and mushroom and cut up finely.

3 Snip bacon into small pieces with scissors.

4 Mix milk, seasoning, egg and grated cheese
  together in a basin.

5 Fry the bacon, onion and mushroom pieces gently in oil until cooked but *not* browned. Add to the milk mixture and stir.

6 Roll pastry thinly on floured table.

7 Using a jam tart cutter, cut out circles of pastry and line patty tins with them.

8 Spoon in enough of the filling to three-quarters fill them.

9 Bake until browned and set firm – approximately 20 minutes.

Cowboy Pies (makes approximately 12)

*Basic quantity shortcrust
pastry*
Small tin baked beans

150g (6oz) sausage meat
Top of the milk to glaze

1 Light oven on Gas Mark 6 (Electricity
   400°F/200°C).

2 Roll pastry thinly and cut 12 circles of pastry,
   using a cutter slightly bigger than the top of the
   jam tart tins.

3 Also cut 12 slightly smaller circles of pastry using
   the cutter one size smaller.

4 Put bigger circles of pastry in tart tins and three-
   quarter fill with sausage meat and a spoonful of
   baked beans.

5 Brush the underside of the small circles of pastry with cold water, and place them on the tarts as lids. (The water helps to stick the two pieces of pastry together.)

6 Snip or cut a hole in the middle of the lid, to allow steam to escape.

7 Brush with top of the milk to glaze.

8 Bake for 20-25 minutes.

Pizza

In Italy, children take slices of pizza for lunch.

Try making small ones to take to school – they are equally nice eaten hot or cold, and can be frozen.

Scone base
150g (6oz) self-raising flour
2.5ml (½ teaspoonful) mustard powder (optional)
A large pinch of salt and pepper
50g (2oz) margarine
60ml (4 tablespoonfuls) milk

Topping

1 medium onion, peeled and chopped
100g (4oz) bacon, snipped into small strips
1 small tin tomatoes (strain off some of juice)
Large pinch of mixed herbs
150g (6oz) grated cheese
12½g (½oz) butter

1 Light oven on Gas Mark 6 (Electricity 400°F/200°C).

2 Grease two baking sheets.

3 Sieve flour and seasoning into mixing bowl.

4 Rub margarine into flour.

5 Add most of milk and mix to a stiff dough using a round-bladed knife. Use rest of milk if needed.

6 Cut into 3 pieces and pat into thin rounds about the size of a small saucer.

7 Place on baking sheets.

8 Melt butter in a frying pan and fry the bacon and onion gently for 3 minutes.

9 Add the tomatoes and herbs, and cook for another 3-5 minutes.

10 Spread the topping on the scone rounds.

11 Sprinkle with grated cheese.

12 Bake for 20-25 minutes until browned.

Serve hot with a green salad, or eat cold for a packed lunch.

Baked Hot Dogs

16 slices from a large loaf

16 thin pork sausages

100g (4oz) butter or margarine

Chutney or mustard

1 Light oven on Gas Mark 6 (Electricity 400°F/200°C).

2 Grease baking tray.

3 Trim off crusts and flatten bread slices with a rolling pin.

4 Spread each piece of bread first with butter and then with chutney or mustard.

5 Put one sausage on each slice of bread and roll up tightly.

6 Put on baking sheet close together and brush with a little melted butter or margarine.

7 Bake for 30 minutes approximately.

8 Eat hot or cold.

Pitta Bread Pouches

Toast Pitta bread (available at delicatessen shops and some supermarkets) in an electric toaster. Cut in half and stuff with filling of your choice, or try chopped salad vegetables and cheese mixed with mayonnaise.

Scotch Eggs

4 hard-boiled eggs
½ beaten egg

200g (8oz) sausage meat
½ pkt golden breadcrumbs

1 Light oven on Gas Mark 6 (Electricity 400°F/200°C).

2 Remove egg shells and rinse eggs in cold water.

3 Divide sausage meat into four pieces and flatten each piece on a floured table with floured fingers.

4 Wrap each egg and mould into a good egg shape, pinching the joins.

5 Roll in beaten egg and then coat in breadcrumbs.

6 Wrap each Scotch egg separately and loosely in a piece of greased foil or greaseproof paper, twisting the ends like a toffee wrapping.

7 Place on baking sheet.

8 Bake for 25-30 minutes.

Scotch eggs may be fried in deep fat for 10 minutes instead of being wrapped and baked, BUT great care must be taken.

Ideas for Salads to serve with Scotch Eggs

Cold boiled rice mixed with chopped celery, salted peanuts and a sprinkling of orange juice.

Shredded lettuce with tomato slices and chopped chives.

Grated eating apple with walnuts and raisins
(a sprinkling of lemon juice will stop the apple
turning brown).

Grated carrot mixed with desiccated coconut.

Shredded white cabbage mixed with salad cream,
grated onion and carrots.

Diced beetroot and cooked new potatoes with plain
yogurt and a sprinkling of chopped parsley.

Cheesy Peanut Biscuits

75g (3oz) plain flour
   (white or wholewheat)
50g (2oz) margarine
50g (2oz) grated cheese
2 large pinches of salt

6 shakes of pepper
1 egg yolk
25g (1oz) chopped
   salted peanuts

Note

A *pinch* of salt means as much as can be held between thumb and one fingertip.

A *large pinch* of salt means as much as can be held between thumb and two fingertips.

1 Light oven on Gas Mark 6 (Electricity 400°F/200°C).

2 Grease baking sheet.

3 Rub fat into flour, salt and pepper.

4 Stir in the grated cheese.

5 Mix to a stiff dough with egg yolk.

6 Roll out on a floured table.

7 Cut into shapes.

8 Brush with egg white, sprinkle with chopped nuts and press in.

9 Place on baking sheet.

10 Bake until browned, approximately 10 minutes.

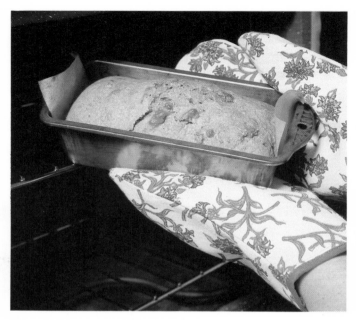

Try a new sort of bread!

Nut Bread

350g (14oz)
  self-raising flour,
  wholewheat or white
100g (4oz) brown sugar
50g (2oz) margarine

100g (4oz) chopped
  walnuts
1 egg
5ml (teaspoonful) salt
250ml (½pt) milk

1 Light oven on Gas Mark 4 (Electricity 350°F/180°C).

2 Grease and line a large loaf tin or two smaller
  loaf tins.

3 Mix flour and salt together, and rub in margarine.

4 Add the sugar and nuts, and stir.

5 Beat the egg and milk together and stir into the other ingredients to make a very soft mixture.

6 Pour into prepared tin.

7 Bake large loaf for approximately 1-1¼ hours.

Bake small loaf for approximately 35 minutes (or only 5 minutes on power 6 in the microwave oven. Remember, do not use a metal tin in the microwave.)

Note: Test with a skewer. If the centre of the loaf is still sticky, bake a little longer.

8 Serve sliced and buttered.

Cheese and Apricot Loaf

350g (14oz) self-raising flour
Large pinch of salt
Large pinch of cayenne
 pepper
Large pinch of dry mustard
75g (3oz) margarine
75g (3oz) mature Cheddar
 cheese, grated
75g (3oz) dried chopped
 apricots (previously soaked
 for ½ hour and drained)
1 egg
250ml (½ pt) milk

Topping

25g (1oz) mature Cheddar
 cheese, grated
25g (1oz) sliced almonds

1 Light oven on Gas Mark 4 (Electricity
 350°F/180°C).

2 Grease and line one large loaf tin, or two smaller
 loaf tins.

3 Sieve flour, salt, pepper and mustard and rub in
 the margarine.

4 Add grated cheese and chopped apricots.

5 Mix in the beaten egg and milk, and beat well.

6 Put into tin and level the surface.

7 Mix the topping ingredients together and
 sprinkle on the surface.

8 Bake the large loaf for approximately 1 hour or until firm to the touch.

Bake smaller loaves for approximately 40-45 minutes.

Or: Microwave for 6 minutes, on power 6 (bake).

9 Turn out onto a cooling tray.

10 Serve sliced and buttered or use to make sandwiches.

Bran Loaf

1 cupful All-Bran cereal
1 cupful sugar
(brown or white)

1 cupful dried fruit
1 cupful milk
1 cupful self-raising flour

1 Light oven on Gas Mark 4 (Electricity 350°F/180°C).

2 Grease a 400g (1lb) loaf tin and line the bottom with greaseproof paper.

3 Put the All-Bran, sugar, fruit and milk all together in a bowl and leave to soak in the milk for 1 hour.

4 Add the flour and stir in thoroughly.

5 Put into tin and smooth the top.

6 Bake for 45-60 minutes. Test with a skewer – if centre of loaf is still sticky, bake a little longer.

Mrs Organ's Ginger Biscuits

(makes 30)

75 g (3 oz) golden syrup (to
  weigh syrup, see page 43)
100 g (4 oz) margarine
75 g (3 oz) caster sugar
150 g (6 oz) self-raising
  flour

10 ml (2 level
  teaspoonfuls) ground
  ginger
Large pinch of
  bicarbonate of soda

1 Light oven on Gas Mark 5 (Electricity 375°F/190°C).

2 Grease two baking sheets.

3 Put flour, ginger and bicarbonate of soda *in* a
  sieve *on* a plate.

4 *Gently* melt syrup, margarine and sugar in a pan.

5 Sieve dry ingredients into pan.

6 Stir, leave to cool for 5 minutes.

7 Make into balls and flatten on baking sheet with
  two fingers.

8 Bake for 10 minutes until golden brown.

9 Transfer to cooling tray whilst still warm, using a
  fish slice.

41

Lemon Slice

100g (4oz) margarine
75g (3oz) brown sugar

125g (5oz) self-raising flour
75g (3oz) coconut

Icing

Juice of 1 lemon
100g (4oz) icing sugar

4 drops yellow food
colouring (optional)

1 Light oven on Gas Mark 4 (Electricity
   350°F/180°C).

2 Grease a Swiss roll tin.

3 Melt margarine *gently* in a pan.

4 Add sugar, coconut and flour.

5 Stir thoroughly.

6 Press into the greased tin using the back of a tablespoon to flatten and smooth.

7 Bake for 15 minutes.

8 Cut up into small squares. DO NOT REMOVE FROM TIN.

9 Mix the icing sugar with the colouring and lemon juice to make a spreading consistency.

10 Pour over the biscuit mixture and smooth with a knife to cover.

11 Remove from tin when cooled and the icing has set.

Chocolate Haystacks (makes 24)

100g (4oz) finely crushed cornflakes

100g (4oz) dried milk powder

25g (1oz) cocoa

100g (4oz) margarine

125g (5oz) golden syrup

(To weigh syrup accurately – weigh a small pan on the scales, and add to that the weight of the syrup needed. Pour the syrup into the pan until the pointer reaches the weight of the two added together.)

1 Grease a baking sheet.

2 Put cornflakes, milk powder and cocoa into a bowl and mix thoroughly.

3 Melt the syrup and margarine gently together in a pan. DO NOT ALLOW TO BOIL.

4 Pour onto dry ingredients and stir together.

5 Using hands, press together into smallish pyramids and put on baking sheet to harden.

TIP To crush cornflakes, put them in a polythene bag and crush with a rolling pin.

Boiled Fruit Cake

125 ml (¼ pt) cold water
100 g (4 oz) sugar
(brown or white)
200 g (8 oz) mixed dried
fruit
200 g (8 oz) self-raising
flour

100 g (4 oz) margarine
5 ml (1 level teaspoonful)
ground mixed spice
1 egg (size 3 or 4)
50 g (2 oz) flaked
almonds

1 Light oven on Gas Mark 4 (Electricity 350°F/180°C).

2 Grease and line the bottom of a 20 cm (8 in)
square tin.

3 Put water, dried fruit and sugar into a pan and
bring to the boil.

4 Turn off heat and leave to cool.

5 Sieve flour and mixed spice into a mixing bowl,
and rub in the margarine until the mixture looks
like breadcrumbs.

6 Add the beaten egg and the cooled fruit mixture
to the other ingredients and stir thoroughly.

7 Put into prepared tin and level the top.

8 Sprinkle on the almonds.

9 Bake until done, when tested with a skewer –
   approximately 45 minutes. (Photo page 37.)

10 Cut into squares when cool.

11 This cake freezes very well.

Melting Moments

*125 g (5 oz) self-raising
   flour*
75 g (3 oz) caster sugar
75 g (3 oz) soft margarine
25 g (1 oz) lard
½ beaten egg (size 3)

*5 ml (1 teaspoonful)
   vanilla essence*
*25 g (1 oz) coconut or
   porridge oats*
6 glacé cherries

1 Light oven on Gas Mark 5 (Electricity 375°F/190°C).

2 Grease two baking sheets.

3 Beat egg in a basin and add the vanilla.

4 Put flour *in* a sieve *on* a plate.

5 Put lard, margarine and sugar in a mixing bowl and beat with a wooden spoon until soft and creamy. Add the egg and beat again.

6 Shake in all the flour and stir to make a stiff dough.

7 Put coconut or oats on a plate.

8 Using your hands, shape marble-sized pieces of the dough then roll them in the coconut or oats.

9 Put on baking sheet and flatten. *Do not put too close together because they spread during cooking.*

10 Press a small piece of cherry in centre of each biscuit.

11 Bake until golden brown – 8-10 minutes. Then, using a fish slice, remove from baking sheet immediately and place on a wire cooling tray.

> **Note** Biscuits are always soft when baked; they go crisp as they cool.

Shortcake Whirls

200g (8oz) soft
  margarine
50g (2oz) icing sugar
200g (8oz) plain flour

A little raspberry jam
and a little extra icing
sugar to decorate

1 Light oven on Gas Mark 4 (Electricity 350°F/180°C).

2 Grease patty tins.

3 Put flour *in* a sieve *on* a plate.

4 Put margarine and icing sugar into a mixing bowl and beat thoroughly with a wooden spoon until *very* soft and creamy.

5 Gradually stir in the flour.

6 Put the mixture into a forcing bag fitted with a large star nozzle.

7 Using a circular motion, pipe whirls of mixture

into greased patty tins, leaving a slight hollow in the centre.

8 Bake until a pale brown – approximately 20-25 minutes.

9 Remove from tins and cool.

10 Sprinkle with icing sugar, using a sieve, and put a little bead of jam into centre hollow of each.

Making up a lunch

If a meal is well balanced, it is just as good cold as it is hot. To be balanced, it should contain a good mixture of foods from each of these groups:

Proteins   meat, fish, eggs, milk, cheese, wholegrain cereals, nuts, peas, beans.

Vitamins and Minerals   fresh fruit and vegetables, milk, red meat, bread, margarine, oily fish.

Carbohydrates   all sugary and starchy foods, such as bread, pastries, etc.

Fats   butter, lard, margarine, oil, etc., and also foods cooked in fat.

Lastly *fibre* is also important, and is found in wholegrain cereal products, bran and bran products, peas, beans, and skins of fruit and raw vegetables.

The new easy to carry lunch boxes are both colourful and strong, and just right for a child's packed lunch.

Plastic food boxes, lidded beakers and containers are easily bought, but the re-usable boxes that icecream and margarine are often packed in are just as good.

Packed meals can only be enjoyable if they are fresh and moist. Pack carefully in foil, cling film or polythene bags.

Many Primary schools only allow children to take the new unbreakable flasks (see opposite).

...d something different each day - packed meals need never be boring!

Index